Contents

What is metal?

Metal is a material.

It is found in the world around us.

Materials

Metal

Cassie Mayer

www.heinemann.co.uk/library
Visit our website to find out more information about Heinemann Library books.

To order:
 Phone 44 (0) 1865 888066
 Send a fax to 44 (0) 1865 314091
 Visit the Heinemann Bookshop at www.heinemann.co.uk/library to browse our catalogue and order online.

First published in Great Britain by Heinemann Library, Halley Court, Jordan Hill, Oxford OX2 8EJ, part of Pearson Education. Heinemann is a registered trademark of Pearson Education Ltd.

© Pearson Education Ltd 2008

Editorial: Diyan Leake
Design: Joanna Hinton-Malivoire
Picture research: Tracy Cummins and Heather Mauldin
Production: Duncan Gilbert

Originated by Chroma Graphics (Overseas) Pte Ltd
Printed and bound in China by South China Printing Co. Ltd

ISBN 978 0 431 19257 4
12 11 10 09 08
10 9 8 7 6 5 4 3 2 1

British Library Cataloguing in Publication Data
Mayer, Cassie
Metal. - (Materials)
1. Metals - Juvenile literature
I. Title
620.1'6

Acknowledgments
The author and publisher are grateful to the following for permission to reproduce copyright material:
© Corbis p. **15** (Steve Hamblin); © Getty Images pp. **4** (Don Klumpp), **14**, **23** bottom (Jim Corwin), **16** (AFP/ Tengku Bahar); © Heinemann Raintree pp. **6**, **8**, **9**, **19**, **20**, **21**, **22** (David Rigg); © istockphoto pp. **12** (Ugur Bariskan), **17** (Marcus Lindström); © Photos.com p. **13**; © Shutterstock pp. **5** (Marek Slusarczyk), **7** (Inta Eihmane), **10**, **23** top (LockStockBob), **11** (Holly Kuchera), **18** (Aceshot1).

Cover image used with permission of © Getty Images (Bryan Mullennix). Back cover image used with permission of © Heinemann Raintree (David Rigg).

Every effort has been made to contact copyright holders of any material reproduced in this book. Any omissions will be rectified in subsequent printings if notice is given to the publisher.

Metal is in rocks.

Metal can be strong.

Metal can be stiff.

What can metal do?

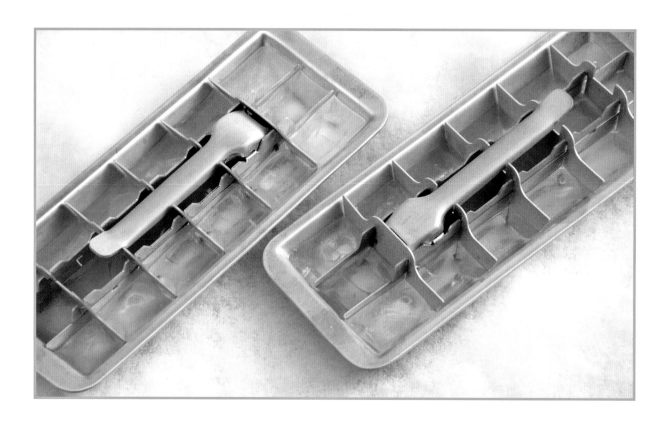

Metal can be made cold.

Metal can be made hot.

What happens when metal is heated?

Metal can be heated.

Metal melts when it is very hot.

When metal is heated, it can be made into a new shape.

After it is heated, metal can cool down again.

Recycling metal

Metal can be recycled.

It can be used to make new
metal things.

Metal can be used to make cars.

Metal can be used to make cans.

How do people use metal?

Metal can be used to build.

Metal can be used to make pots
and pans.

Lots of food comes in metal cans.

Metal can be used to make lots
of things.

Things made of metal

◀ tin foil

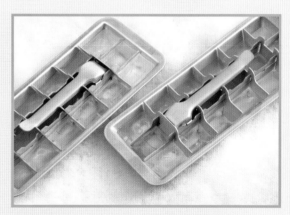

▲ ice cube trays

▲ pots and pans

Picture glossary

melt change from a solid into a liquid. Metal is a material that melts when it is heated.

recycle take old things to make them into new things

Content vocabulary for teachers

natural material material from plants, animals, or within the earth that can be used by people

Index

Notes for parents and teachers

Before reading   Put items made of materials such as wood, plastic, metal, and rubber in a closed bag. Challenge the children to feel in the bag and, without looking, identify the object made of metal. What did it feel like? Was it cold to touch? Was it heavy? Talk about the properties of metal.

After reading

- Show the children some lengths of metal and wood. Then put both in a fridge. Ask the children to predict how the materials will feel after they have been in the fridge for one hour. After an hour, take out the metal and the wood and encourage the children to talk about how they feel. Then put the metal and the wood on a window sill in the sun. After a while pass around the wood and the metal. Talk about which is warmer.
- Scatter some paperclips on to a piece of card. Move a magnet around under the card and watch the paperclips move. Talk about how some metal is magnetic.